$2—

As Is

Y0-AER-014

poetry £

12/14 B

1998

Escape of the Bird Women

Linda Andrews

Escape of the Bird Women

Blue Begonia Press • Yakima, Washington

Acknowledgments

"My Daughter in the Surf," *Cumberland Poetry Review*
"When a Daughter is Missing," *Calyx*
"Sleepless," *Image*
"Desert East of Home," *mud creek*
"Badlands, Sheep Mountain Table," *Prairie Winds*
"For the Long Distance Rider," *Nimrod*
"True Story of the Bird Women," *Willow Springs*
"Escape of the Bird Women," "Two Hearted River" and
"Embrace," *Poetry Northwest*
"Farms" and "Temporary Shelters," *Alaska Quarterly Review*
"Late August Daybreak," *Northwest Poets and Artists Calendar*, 1990
"October Orchard," *Northern Lights*
"Greuor Farm," *Midwest Quarterly*
"Downwind," *West Wind Review*
"The Bathers," *Northwest Poets and Artists Calendar*, 1993
"Late Sky," "All the Calliopes in Montana," "Plains at Belle
Fourche," "Io, One Summer," and "The Bathers," *Gaia*
"Parthenogenesis," "Trajectory of the Lost," and "When a Daughter
is Missing" received the Academy of American Poets prize,
University of Washington, 1991.
"Io, One Summer," "Invitation" and "Embrace" received the
Vernon M. Spence Prize for Poetry, University of Washington, 1992.

My thanks to the Ucross Foundation for a summer fellowship, during
which some of these poems were written.

Special thanks to Judith Skillman for her steady encouragement and
constant friendship.

Cover photograph of Linda Andrews by Daniel Lamberton.
Cover painting, *Downwind*, by Randy LeSage.

ISBN: 0-911287-25-6
Book design by Karen and Jim Bodeen
Blue Begonia Press   225 S. 15th Ave.   Yakima, WA 98902-3821

For Carrie, Jason, Daniel

Table of Contents

Part I

Part II

Part III

Part IV

Part I

Tonight, I aim this dream straight at your skull
While you nestle it against soft feathers

David Wagoner

The Gray Women

"...had only one eye and one tooth
among them, which they would share."
Edith Hamilton, *Mythology*

One eye is enough.
Prophecies are fulfilled
off stage, in the dusk that lies
on all sides of us. One tooth is enough
for sucking water out of the mist,
our lips like sponges.

It's our hands we couldn't do without,
to pass the eye and tooth among us.
Hands to feel the soul
of the gray water sliding
through our land. With hands
we can hold ourselves upright,
scratching in the tree bark
for fingerholds.

The great joke is our wings, our swan
silhouettes. Wings—in a place where the mist
deepens and the green vines
are inescapable. You might expect us then
to use the wings to hide
our faces, our shrinking bodies.

But gray from birth,
we have nothing to fear.
Withering is not painful and makes it easier
to share the eye and tooth. We've been spared
the drowning details of vanity, the burden
of seduction.

But the moon wavers past
and never seeing us against this gray land
leaves us bereft of daughters.

Knowing Lilith

We could be her daughters
and she knows where we live.

For evidence: my black hair and the way
you never sleep, one daughter born

with two wraps of cord around her neck
and yours, bubbling in her red pool.

There was Eve, but first there was Lilith,
refusing domination, living in a cave.

She could change the shape of her body
and we have tried this, fattening for birth

or for happiness. We have ached
with these changes but are glad

that at least we are not made like Eve,
a woman with perfect hands

who sleeps in lotion and gloves
and reaches for her lover

with the touch of cotton,
always cotton.

We have sold and re-sold our bodies:
when imagination failed,

we married. And, though we tried to be quiet,
the argument Lilith began with Adam

kept coming out of our mouths.
Love someone

for his goodness and beauty.
He will set about proving you wrong.

My Daughter in the Surf

She's impatient with the froth
that licks at her legs
and wants to float on the surface
tension, the clear green swells.
A series of curves moves toward her,
deep troughs in between.
Swells hold themselves up,
pose transparent, innocent,
like a magician holding up
empty hands to lure belief.
I'm afraid of the wave
that could take her
under its watery skin
and hold her in suspension
like a strap of seaweed.

It's better for now that she stretch
in the warm pebbled space
between the ocean and myself.
It's too early to tell her
of wave crest slipping into trough.
As the moon rises in her,
I'm destined to be the lesser pull.
But for now she explores the beach
and to the depths of my pocket
trusts her treasures—
a green stone
that could be jade or the color of the sea
compressed into rock,
a spiraled shell that must have come
from a tiny unicorn,
and a rock that balances
the tension of opposites
in its white and black bands.

Trajectory of the Lost

> "Remember these things lost; under the vaulting roof
> of the cathedral, burn a candle to the memory."
> Francois Leydet, *Time and the River Flowing*

Whether they've been thrown or dropped
or carefully laid aside doesn't matter. Once
they escape, try tears. Pleading. Nonchalance.
All are of no consequence to the curved path
of things hurtling through space.

This time, call the lost one
a daughter. I insist
she is lost, though a woman tells me,
There is nothing lost
in God's kingdom. We just don't know
where she is.

What I learn is that the lost
are presumed found by numbers. I'm told to speak
by weight, height, birth time. Be glad
she has braces. Nothing lost in God's kingdom,
we just don't know that at the end
of the litany comes the official case number
that pretends to know a child.

If I get her back, I'll drape her
in the chains of her own innocence, take her
to the yellow kitchen and our fragrant division of labor
that becomes her favorite food. It begins to seem
that the found and the lost
divide the world.

The tamest body
harbors its own freedom, like one red shirt

hanging in the closet. Maybe she's gone to find
the secret train that runs through her city. Or to submit
to a threat to fall under someone's wheels.

If this were a simple geometry, her path
could be called a curve that cuts all of a given family
of curves at the same angle. Small things have happened
since she left: her cat became a father;
they've put a guard rail along the cliff
that always frightened her.

The Running Girl

> "Most reckless things are beautiful in some way...."
> John Ashbery

She shaved her head for speed, a black coat
her sail, as if on a spinnaker reach down-
wind to the darkest water.

The first time she ran was through heavy rain, headed
for a house she was sure had no rules, where lights
and music would burn all night and her answering body
could heat through with freedom. Child, it was January
and their fire turned out to be from the thinnest match.
It would have taken days for you to dry, the leaden coat
anchoring you to the floor.

For thrills: cigarettes, the ash flicked into a lit circle
of pavement, a cement landscape the wind never stirs,
small change deep in the pocket of her coat, the coat gotten
in street trade, hanging long, shabby and seeming weighted
at the bottom like tired drapes.

From then on, she was gone and brought back. Gone again,
held away from home by the dark sleeve of night, by burrowing dogs,
ventriloquists, mask makers, or whoever makes threats come true.
Whoever heard of such things: a poppy scraping its own petals
against a brick wall, a horse wrapping itself in barbed wire,
a bee daring itself to be eaten by the dog.

When a Daughter is Missing

> "The answer to my prayer may require a miracle...."
> from the Unfailing Prayer to St. Anthony

Say you want your daughter back, covered
by innocence. Say you want her
recovered in time.

The impossible distance of these things can send you
to drop again onto your knees in front of a flaming
bank of candles, your thin coins
clinking into the leaded box. The flames
light your skin, pull you back to when faith
was untested and beauty was as simple
as the gilt edge of a holy card.

And while you kneel with all desires trickling
out of your heart, your far-flung girl carries
her desire with her, broadcasts it
to the streets, and any taker/any giver
will do. She never learned the fine art
of repression, never learned to hold it
all in the heart, the reservoir of want.

When a daughter is missing, every swollen
river and ditch running full
becomes a possible carrier of bones.
A walk in the woods is impossible.
And in the city, you imagine her footprints
on all the crumbling sidewalks.

If days continue
to come and go, the question becomes
how to count them. She's come to know
alarming people, the seduction of jive. She's gone

courting, but whether for tongue or knife blade,
we don't know.

When a daughter is missing, you believe equally
that the thing you fear has happened or
is about to happen. Everywhere
other women walk with their children.

At This Hour

The man at the edge of the world lies
reading in his bed, in a line with all

the other men wrapped in rags and concrete.
They're safe enough from high tide

but everything else seems possible—broken glass,
quick rain, hungry dogs. He reads at midnight

by light trapped in the lobby at his back.
What voices rise off his page, out here

on the sidewalk, while all the other men
snore it off. Past his feet, the ferries

ride the sheen of the bay, bringing who
at this hour—those desperate for fish

at the all-night stand? a woman in labor trying
to reach the hospital? They cut a path

through the salt to the reader. They bring with them
no change of weather. His pages do not rustle

and the book is not swept out of his hands.
It is as peaceful as it gets.

Sleepless

for the Jean Paul Sartre
Memorial NO EXIT Rooming House, Seattle

We've all stayed here
at one time or another
and taken a turn at the window
staring into the yellow light.

Someone else's jazz
winds through the rooms
and out into the dead end street.
The house pulses and becomes
one of the chambers of the heart.
The one that last fills.
No handsome sleepers here.

But in your time you've gotten
used to this living
among unaccustomed furniture
and the cunning cobweb.
There's been time enough
even for camellias
to learn how to vine
and tangle at the juncture
of the north and west walls.

The spent blooms
hang like paper decorations
where you stand at the window,
holding back the strip of curtain.
The lover meant to rescue or torture
may soon wander down this dead end.
It will be by mistake.
The way we all think we first arrived.

Late Sky
at Bend, Oregon

Sunset, and the high desert sky breaks
into bands: black, midnight blue,
sea green and yellow. Colors of the desert
thrown into the sky like a scarf.

Black predominates:
the color of recent violence.
Tubes of lava run for miles
below the crust and inside,
the most a lantern will show
is the cloud of a child's breath
or small patch of cave wall.
All that can be done
is trust the dark floor shaped in waves,
ridges of tide from a solid sea.

Midnight blue well before midnight,
the band of sky just dark enough for stars:
pool of ink, or a lover's eyes
steadfast and deep.
The stars begin here,
faint jagged shapes
left behind for us to navigate.

Sea green. Before mountains,
the sea rolled through here.
For proof, tiny skeletons
embedded in sandstone
or this too-earthly green in the night sky
and in the noble fir,
needles whirled on the stems.
Each year's growth goes

seamlessly into the next.
Yellow, the last color
to outline the mountains,
palest layer of the sky, aretes
backlit as if by a last candle.
Silhouettes glow and seem to close in,
collapsed craters and cinder cones
in a chain scattered
like black sleeping hearts.

Part II

The phoebe flew back and forth
between the fencepost and the tree—
not nest-building, just restless...

Jane Kenyon

The Desert East of Home

The fall light is white as summer heat,
strong enough to purify
three generations of tumbleweed.
The young one is green,
a spiky pink cup at each node.
Last season's brush is pure gold,
not alive but not quite seeming dead;
more glowing with memory or anticipation.
The oldest is skeletal, gray and sparse.
Freed of its blooms,
it's barely attached to the sand,
waiting for the courtship
of a fast fall wind to send it tumbling.

Our sun rises from this place
and west of the mountains
we live in its reflection,
study our children's faces
by secondary light.
This land isn't barren, but fallow,
unmated by the rain we keep for ourselves.
This clear light shows
the fine crazing around our eyes.
Once home, we'll pat them smooth
with rain soaked hands.

Parthenogenesis

Anesthesia

He invites her to compose herself along the lines
of a favorite dream and he slides her, suspended,
into the gray light. This sleep is quick. Her body
will be his. For consolation, she is told to imagine
one loved place and not think about the coming
of her own bright blood.

He takes her without assurance, the mixture
dripped into her veins a product of his belief
and past success, or failure. She has authorized him
to act in her best interest and under his tutelage
she passes through every artist she loves, becomes the butterfly
and then is gone.

Surgery

He opens her along a thin red seam, and finds a private dark
she never knew she had, one of the various truths
the mature body still holds for surprise.

And the surgeon can't, in fact, tell the woman why
her body did this, why the ovum would take its solitary urge
toward life this far. A bleeding into a secret
interior pocket. Desire is not listed as a possible cause.

Analysis

This is truly the body undressed. Nothing sings
through this organ anymore, not desire

or pain. Not even blood. What has been taken
from her has been slashed for examination
and it twists in the gray liquid and flutes
like a chanterelle.

There are other things that women have made.
Roses have grown inside them, petals arched back
with longing, the color gone from red to chocolate
with age and waiting. Blood held with no escape.

Recovery

Call these vagaries by their scientific names,
hide them in small containers
labeled in a dead language. Refrigerate
to the limit of their shelf life and finally
throw them out for lack of interest.
Let these ghost flowers precede us by decades
to the ash heap.

The Artificial Heart

By the time they're done with me, I'll have a pendulum
in my chest, need to be wound, and will chime
every last hour. Such simple science appeals,
since living with my toxic self has brought me
like a bride to a wedding with technology.

I know it's gone faint and sometime, but I will miss
the sound of my own heart. Soon I will whir and click,
send power across my skin from the battery
tucked in a pouch under my arm. In these
last days as myself, I wonder if their machine

will work in the dark, wrapped in the softness
of the body. Surely their cool, impervious
heart will have its required flaw, or suffer
a whole fist full of flaws. Or maybe it is perfect
and the rest of me will wash up rusty and rough

against its gleaming shore. Remember
how they told us: our childish hearts
could fit in our palms and God could look in
our throbbing souls to see how we had sinned.
My living heart too clearly tells the way I've lived

and shows itself to be the blind corner of a lifetime,
the convergence of past and present tense, its thick
walls betraying my narrow purchase on the world.
I wonder if their heart will pump once they've thrown
my used one out or if I'll be seduced

by a sudden fatal rhythm. At home, something's gone
wrong with the fridge. A haze of frost lies on
the celery. Eggs have broken on their own,
a clear and yellow mist frozen
on to their basket.

The Offering

at Bowman Bay

Left alone here on this midnight beach is a statue
of a woman said to be unremarkable
in the daylight. But she is huge and holds up
that fish, that offering.

The man and woman circling her cause
this change again and again: from maiden
to fish woman, hair becoming a river of kelp
down her back, skirt falling away
in favor of scales carved deep into her sides, feet
widening into fins. Through her ruined body
she stands half-sister to herself.

The story says she gave her body to the sea
so her people would always have salmon.
Her catch held high,
the waves approve and since they have no roses,
fling bits of net and seaweed at her feet.

The surface of the world wavers toward her
with gifts and pulls away. Drift logs
are the beached ribs of whales and kelp
coils like quiet snakes. The beach is her jewel box
and the surf drags its phosphorescent voice through the pebbles,
hissing of diamonds and gravel. How many times has she stood
witness to floods and abandon, forced to watch what beats forth
from the world's indifferent heart.

She's caught in the act of sacrifice
as if she had done nothing else with her life
but give it away. The man and woman
walk back to the small cabin
jutting into the forest on stilts. Other nights he will sit
alone on the logs, soaked up like the diamonds and haunted.

Turquoise

At first, the blue stones reminded her only
of the Welsh vicar who had given her
the necklace, saying, *This belonged
to my mother; take it with you as you go
and keep to the road that brought you.*

The silver beads and blue stones
of the dead woman crossed oceans and became
what a different man liked to save for last
when undressing the traveler. Later,
and this was no longer an accident,
the same blue was spotted at the museum
in the Purification Series:

twelve panels, and from other canvasses
stunned birds watched, as calf and chalice
burned and congealed and became
what they had not been before,
with the implication for the traveler:
Carry nothing.

There are no wildflowers this turquoise,
nor is it found in the human eye. Paint
your rooms this color and risk
going mad against the walls.

All the Calliopes in Montana

As if they were children, all the calliopes in Montana
have been carried to one old room. Inside a glass
and cherry wood cabinet rests a violin that, for fifty cents,
will play.

For fifty cents
a melody will coil out
into the museum. And part of the chorus, one minor
progression of notes, pulls them up to the curved
glass. And they're sure they know the tune or
his grandmother sang it to him or they need to hold on
to it to stay in love.

Resined wheels sing the wires of the violin, a hill
of powder collecting below the neck. And the instrument
is lit from below, lit with pleasure and past, paid as it is
to remember missing melodies. How hard it would be—all this
remembering of sound, as difficult as resurrecting a mother's laugh,
grandfather's salute down a long table, or the voice
of someone who once loved you.

And the man and woman can't pretend they didn't start this
with their pooling of quarters. But then the whirring
took over, the eerie progression of notes that had them staring
through the glass as into a crystal ball,

had them wanting their arms around each other
and they did. Had them wanting to dance
and they didn't. Even though the floorboards would
have groaned with them and the dust would
have parted for them, they didn't dance
but kept their balance, so the melody retreats
and won't be recollected, taking the brittle invitation
deep into the machine fallen dark.

Plains at Belle Fourche

South Dakota

Ahead, the sky is spilling itself
        upon the plains, from a blue-gray
theatre curtain, hung with rips of lightning.

I'm too far away for the sound
        of thunder. Here, it's all wheat ruffling
in the first wind, crickets filling

the ditches with falsetto voice. The decision—
        whether to drive into the chaos or let it
come to me. The first rondels of rain hit

and the crickets mostly fall quiet. Starlings
        thick on the barbed wire of the cattle pen
lift off. Even the cows begin to notice

and start their useless noise. The curtain
        is sweeping this way. In the dreams
of Midwestern girls, such storms can narrow

quickly down to funnels, like an angry
        father surging up the driveway, come
to terrorize the ones who love him.

Rain harder now and more wind. Growing up
        with thunder and lightning
gets you ready for anything. It trains you

to see ditches, underpasses, or a deep crease
        in the earth as shelter. For anyone new
to tornados, I would tell them this:

They are beautiful.
        When your storm comes close

find a low place in the earth. Then set

your back to the funnel and let it sweep
        your house away.
Watch it as long as you can.

Burning the Fields

Imagine setting fire to what you love.

Even for the sake of fertility this is a harsh flare
and, overtaken by the burn, grasshoppers
snap open, dragonflies turn
inside out.

Flames run for the ditch. Even the fence—
barbed wire wedded to wood—chars black
and seems a deep rest on a sheet
of orange music.

Across the field, the farmer's face and cowboy hat
float above the fire and, upwind from the smoke,
cows graze unaware that farmers can find
such drastic solutions.

Starlings perch thick on the wire, black as ash,
until they lift on one wing toward the poplars
and catch there as if in some crazy woman's hair.
Skeins of smoke drift up.

What remains is the curve of the land, the farmer
and the singed promise of a clean start.

Badlands

These places without water are easy to love
        since the way the land's made is clear, full
with the irony of ancient seas.

Salt traces the corners of your eyes and proves
        your own internal sea. You are turning inside out and begin
to feel the possibility of falling to dust.

There are teeth scattered through the clay—three-pointed
        ancient teeth black from manganese. Your fingers sift the dust
and small bones, and you begin to know

what it would be like to lie down here, become thin
        and brown, and finally leave your jaw
as someone's future treasure. If the earth can so brazenly

show its mountings and curves, the least you can do
        is let your bones shine through your skin,
become as clean as the rocks and leave movement

up to the wind. You're pure as the land
        when you feel your last swallow of water travel
your throat and get down to the act of disappearing.

Badlands—Sheep Mountain Table

It went like this, my love. The road led up
        a tableland, a table set
with all we'd ever need—wild wheat waving
        and juniper berries green as jade.

The high grassland is one bouquet—tall grasses
        tinged with pink and the wild sunflowers
you love. They've left your farm by June, but here
        are August sunflowers, as if they've traveled

east all summer to be here. The roads are white dust,
        pulverized clay soft as the finest talc, and trail off
through the grass. Remember we had talked about
        becoming dust together?

This matte world affords no reflections, no shadows
        or disclaimers and such deep thirst
makes the ground beautiful, breaks it
        into soft white tiles. Beyond this ledge,

the earth is worn in fantastic shapes, clay spires,
        deep white crevices. If surrender to a great force
makes you beautiful, this deadend may finally be
        the catspaw that moves me along.

If you were here, I'd wear a flimsy skirt
        the wind would help you lift,
and a gauze shirt no better than a promise.
        I'd show you my fears

one last time, and let you see the striate rock
        mimic my own flawed skin. The only
hiding place would be the wheat

and enough sky to meet the farthest horizon.

This place would spend its secrets on us, the pure
        light working till we'd bleached free
of our skin. These roads
        that end abruptly, end.

For the Long Distance Rider

> If the horses feel their reins held by a weaker hand,
> they will run wildly out of their course
> and set the earth on fire.
>
> Myth of Phaethon

Having made it past them all eighteen times,
the Lion, Archer and Dog Star,
your magic has distilled down
to a few potions to carry on the way.
What elements your horse needs you learn
by the taste of her sweat. In another land
you would weave her snowshoes
from winter rice straw. But your voice moves her
and she would follow you in the dark,
even if the snow fell deep here.

Don't listen
when I tell you I'm innocent.
I once crossed a pasture and tried walking away.
The roan behind me broke into a trot, his hooves
beat the dirt, the shock of it in my feet. He's upon me
and his soft nose pushes hard
into the hay in my arms. No matter
that it was meant for another, I'm against the fence
and he leads with a muzzle so soft
that I'm fooled into thinking I could go back for more.

It's true that the payment is fire.
The pasture turned to ash
and we've starved every day since.

The True Story of the Bird Women

"A particular goddess
in a certain shape and color
will lead the yogin to understand
the emptiness and illusory nature of his own body."
Seeing With the Mind's Eye

Sailors ride the seas to find a voice
that says *the journey is over.*
You can lie down here.
And if they are busy with sails
and miss the beckoning the first time,
watch them come around again.

Even though we're chained to a rock,
we've been given a voice and must sing.
And until they hear us, they don't know how badly
they want to beach themselves and escape
the dictums of the gods. Until this island,
they sail convinced of the weight
of their cargo and goodness.

They are sick of conquest and our music is just
the lie we must tell for them to know. Stand with me
on this rock and watch the artist in his black boat
flounder toward shore, his final inspiration.

He wants this.
For proof, watch him tumble
toward us in the surf, white skin gleaming
through his useless clothes, his face
glad and frightened, growing younger
behind his beard.

Escape of the Bird Women

By the time he finds his way to us, the sailor
is bled clear and crusted with salt. We are told to know him
by the sins he chose, the ones he was drawn to
as if seeing his own child's face
in a crowd. They are the dares he took,
his coming to this island only the last of them.

He thought we would be slim, hoped to count
our ribs and dream that the true heart
lies just beneath. But our beaks taper down
to points smaller than the pupils
of his eyes. He was so distracted
by the feathers, and craved the plumes
for other seductions and the quills to record the conquests.

Didn't he know, that if the plumage were real
we would fly
to where a man and a woman can be alive
at once. Shelter would be found
in flesh rather than driftwood. Grateful,
we would re-learn the shocks
of human life—
that milk is thin and deceptively blue
and the earth's curve is finally carried
in the spine.

Part III

...feeling the dry soft grass beneath her feet for the first time now...

Jorie Graham

Invitation

This is where the day turns over. After chores
the yellow light bleaches gray. Afternoon rain
shows nothing can be done
to tidy the world. It will be lush
in spite of us.

Near the barn the peacock fans and shudders
his hundred feathered eyes. I'm told
that if he were human, he'd be criminal
with his indiscriminate display.
He quakes easily for goslings
and for his own reflection in chrome.
Soft brown peahens are incidental to the dance.

There have been days of birdsong on this farm
and April nests—hills of pale eggs in the maple,
mud hollows and brown eggs near the pond.
And the peacock, before anything
can hatch or fly, insists
it start again, his iridescent ritual blocking
the path, single eyes shaken loose
and staring up from the grass.

A man once picked the feathers up
and handed them, unsuspecting, to a woman. Something
about the green. Something about the shimmer.

Farms

From the air, the moss-ridden earth
and single farm below seem to contend
that wisdom comes easier
in isolation. Out here, there is no
confusion of roads and no signs
whatsoever. Every road
I've ever taken is below
in the geometry of farms—corduroy earth
set in diamonds and triangles, rivers
through it all wind their sloppy path.

My dear, there are singular curves below, the Missouri
twisting back and forth to be sure it hasn't left
anything within its reach untouched. And that
might be part of the story—determining one's range,
the scope of curves, the orbit of the hips. Winter glaze
lies lightly on the world, the craquelure of ice showing
what belongs to water. The river coursing through
tidy farmland looks like passion's lovely surge.

The plane swings through the sun
and, off the end of the wing, a train pulls
its burden like past lives or wishes fallen
into disrepair. The train pulls on like a man
trudging toward the blessing of an unearned kiss.
I want to ask you why precision and fruitfulness
go together out here, and how a tractor
can come to a perfect point in the furrows
of its own making and still find its way home.

For the Cartographer

These are slow times for the map maker, the world
having gone so blunt with purpose. But still he looks
for the piece of land not yet paced, the unknown
stretch, the space not yet filled with sure things
like mileposts or children.

In the middle of his own land, in the tall grass,
is a yellow house. A dark-haired woman
watches him from the window as he steps
and measures to the end of their plot.
He comes to the same conclusion, always,

that the pieces are locked together, and returns
to tell her in new ways how they belong
to this slow, dry land.
When he leaves again in the morning,
she writes down his story from the night before.

Some day it will all be his, this yellow box
of stories, and they will read as if new,
about the two who started over
even though all around them the world
had been settled and quiet.

49

Late August Daybreak

Easier to render than the straight line,
the curve.

The hose winds through the grass,
water arching out of the sprinkler
as from a gracious hand.
Roots tangle pulpy and white
in the dark earth.
And the hammock hangs
slack from the remembered weight
of a good man at midnight.

The yard itself
will submit to being rectangle,
but not flat.
It slides down toward daybreak
and the pink light that rises
from the meadow,
up from behind the two mares,
their patient breath curling
toward the leftover moon.

Dew falls on the mares equally,
slicks them both, condenses
and runs off their flanks,
glitters last where it disappears
into the ground.

Io, One Summer

"You need not be afraid to enter the dim forest where beasts
crouch in the dusky ravines, for am I not here to protect you?"
Zeus to Io

If she has a failing, it is this: her belief
in words. One beautiful sentence can last her
a year. His mouth on her, his tongue trails the beginnings
of stories, stories that will spring up out of her while
he is gone. He holds her tighter than most mortals
could tolerate and says the truth, *You would let me*
break you. And she counters with the truth,
You already have.

In the careful rhythms of love, she will learn
his body and they will tell each other where
all the scars have come from. He tells her such stories:
of a farm, the drive lined with poplars; of a small city
where hawthorns grow to sixty feet and droop heavy
from hot pink bouquets pinned to their branches;
of another land between their two homes, a place
of headwaters and hot springs, vast enough
to shelter them from a jealous wife.

What remains is their time to travel. She spends
seven days with him going from Garnet to Wraith Hill
and the circle they make is made of every rise and fall:
the taste of his summer skin, the frantic give and take
of love, and every morning she settles herself over him.
On this mountain top is where they should stay, the man and woman
that they are, skins gleaming. The air will thinly cushion them
and the bears can come and take what they want, walk away
with parts of them trailing red from their mouths.

Cows come at nightfall and watch over
what is left. Five white cows sit and feed on moonlight

[handwritten marginalia: His tongue on her tongue]

[handwritten marginalia: Lamberton Ranch? Sunny]

[handwritten marginalia: Why Five?]

and pale grass, smitten by the people in their care,
till sometime toward morning the cows forget and are gone.
The lovers are left against the black sky at the beginning
of morning, balanced between red sunrise and full moon-set.

October Orchard

From here, we take the apples on faith.
It's an orchard because I believe you
and symmetry is telltale,
even from this distance.
The lines of order begin and end
at the random evergreens—
soft crowns of apple trees
in the half leaf of October.

There must be a man and woman over there
as bent and fruitful as their trees.
Strong sons.
Migrant pickers gone elliptically south
by way of onions and potatoes.
Maybe the orchard is creased by gullies,
apples sluiced down toward market.
A few left hanging like lanterns
for winter birds.

Each variety calls a different green
or gold to its leaves and from here
the sections look like states on a map
or mosaic in grain from the county fair.
Once home, we take the whole orchard on faith,
apples on our tables as proof of miracles.

Greuor Farm
North Wales

No prettier place to die, he says
and shows me to my room.
Near deaf, near eighty
he tells stories
and doesn't bother about listeners.

Sixty-five acres and a river.
A house that looks sturdy
from the road. Up close it seems
as though the sea moved through here once
and the walls barely resisted.
Thin, concave at the ceiling,
they bulge from midpoint to floor
like a softly sagging belly.

At the top of the house is my room,
where the walls are most brittle
and the moonlight comes
only as far as the windowsill.
The land is seven colors of slate
and the air in here an inky cobalt,
as thickly blue as the plates
lining the walls.

The old man says there must be sadness
in traveling alone, then leaves.
Under my window
his son rakes sweet grass
for the cow.
And if he came up here
smelling of hay and moonlight
I'd ask him to speak Welsh,
to tell me the story
of how the sea and Mount Snowdon
are held for now in place,
tolerating the passage of travelers
and possible witnesses.

When the moon lets go
sea and slate will meet,
perhaps along the fault at Greuor Farm,
perhaps inside these temporary walls
already shaped for surrender.

Temporary Shelters

•

Again this afternoon, a disc of crows
circles the woods. They seem a hovering
roulette wheel, coming up black, coming up
winter every time in the game of hot or cold.
In this simple equation, if they are here
by thousands, it is winter, bare trees
glorious with crows. There's a shock value
to absolute black against opalescent sky,
their voices shouting us down. Call it
a rookery or canopy of wings.

•

On an island of small houses, this
is one of the smallest, a place
to roost for a season and *begin*
life from the zero as the immigrant said,
living in a simple room where simple things are done.

•

From these sweet interludes hang
the weight of the rest. Like my father, looking
suddenly unlike himself and wistful, mentioning
Belgium, the end of the war, a nurse and a small statue
of a lost child/king found pissing in the snow.

•

There comes a night when you try to sleep in an island lean-to

of wood ribs and thick plastic, a heavy door you slide
into place. There is something in the dark knocking against,
no, throwing itself against, your invisible roof. Pine cones.
But they fly too often and land too hard for a windless
night. Perhaps a demon has followed you home then changed
his mind and is trapped in this bubble with you, no keyhole
for escape. The light comes up and a dark leaf
seems to cut across the space. Whether it was pine cone
or demon, it's now a brown bird sitting on the sill, you
in a birdcage perched on rocks above dark waves.

·

Bought at auction for twenty-five cents, a packet
of love letters from the last century. William writes,
    You may think you can be happy without me, but
    if you are ever untrue to me, the black ghosts of Hell
    will haunt you through life. Their horrible voices
    will echo and re-echo down the dark caverns
    of your passing. Your pleasures will turn to miseries,
    even the flowers will fade and die at your touch
    and birds will cease singing at the approach
    of your footfall. My precious little darling, do not
    let them take you from me for I love you.

·

Here's a snapshot of my parents, newly met
at the Palmetto Lounge, flamingos painted
on the wall behind them, my father still in uniform,
his cap tilted in the way she liked, my mother
leaning into him, smiling, wearing rhinestones, her hair
rolled into a frame for her face.

Downwind

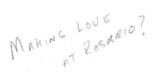

Last night I swam toward you. The water
was black as sleep and I rolled through the swells
toward your shore.

Closing the distance was as simple
as throwing myself in the outgoing tide.
The only lights were the quarter moon,
the phosphorescent outline of my body
and the lamp in your cabin window, a cool
hundred miles downwind.

All signs were favorable: the kelp waving, whales
like soft buoys to mark the channel, night birds
wrapped in speed screaming back at the wind. Soon
gravel underfoot and the heavy climb
back onto the earth.

Sparks were rising from your chimney—you were burning
my roof again. The truckful of old shingles you brought
from my house to yours were still rising through the forest
one by one. With me, the wood was shelter, heavy
and responsible. Here, it's airborne, incandescent
in the crazy science of turning stability to tinder.

I'm washed clean from my long sail. Let us start over,
your green shirt wrapped around me.

The Drowning of Waitsburg

In the dark they wade across the road—
a woman lit by the white bundle
in her arms, the man visible
by the tip of his cigarette.

Behind them, their house is turning
unrecognizable. The back porch tips
into the flood, stairs go soft and surrender,
and a slurry of mud whispers across
their blue floor and says, *Take your baby
and your habits and get out.*

So it has said, house by house,
each high ground temporary and futile.
Leave because the flood has work to do.
There are floor boards to be buckled
and mud to be driven into every crack,
light sockets silted full. By the time you return,
there will be fish under your bed and you see
that the water has pressed itself against your walls,

the way you measured your son every birthday
to see how he'd grown. In two days, the flood grew
six years. How long does it take to scrub the silt
from the skin of a family? Your daughter
will never stop saying that her room
smelled like mushrooms and

her doll buggy must have floated away.
Still now, the streets have forgotten
where they came from, and point neither
east nor west, but simply downstream.

Part IV

A nest—and this we understand right away—
is a precarious thing, and yet it sets us to daydreaming of security.

Gaston Bachelard

Rescue

> "The prospect of rescue undoes you."
> Norman Rush, *Mating*

And then he offers—
I'll take you away from this place where the cold
burns a million holes in the black sky, where the wind
blows so fierce the trees all bend like weak women.
He reminds me there are snakes here and the most common
form of life is cheatgrass.

I know that stars fall all the time,
cows go down and horses are killed by lightning.
I know that we're born from water and to live where it's dry
seems perverse. But I worry that in safe places
you can't see storms coming. Out here I can lie down,
hear my heart pound and know it does more
than keep me alive.

Once I followed a red road through the grassland.
I left home to come here, a string of heartbreak songs
on the radio. I felt as brave as a rented car, a fist
full of cash and a tank of gas can make you.

Now birds land on my porch and don't know
I sit with them. Deer graze while I read,
as if I've gone invisible or lost my scent.
The roads through straw hills teach something
about contrast. What happens is this:
you begin to mistake the red dirt roads
for the veins leading to your heart.

I admit I've been happy. After nights and nights
of being with him, I walk no where. I sashay,
made of liquids. But how could he give me
the Braille of the zodiac over the Bighorns

or the big bass not yet caught in Piney Creek.

I think I'd hold it against him
if I never again saw the sky this way—
the Milky Way like a pale scarf and the Big Dipper
ladling a million smaller stars. I couldn't leave here,
even if he promised me that each day
we'd lie down in kindness.

Homage to a Distant Farm

When islands of garnet saplings rise from the prairie
and sage grows tall enough to hide in with a horse, I'll know
I'm there, finally arrived at the distant farm where a man
lived his life so blond and strong that neither trait
will ever leave him.

What can I tell you about this place before
I've seen it. The promise is that it's been quiet
for forty years, boy stories still roaming
the land. But roaming with a voice that sets
the young trees waving like whips.

There will be one stag among the cattle, brambles caught
in his antlers. Snakes come to drink, undulating
over the repetitions of white granite. And when the poplars
shed, topaz splinters pave the walk.

This land knows the grand gesture, poised
as it is on the cusp of a new moon. The man is also poised.
Whichever way he moves, two women will shiver.
He's come back to the farm to sleep
in the arms of the maple, the lucky one folded with him.

WHO IS THE OTHER WOMAN?

DANS EX?

The Bathers

Come together in a city neither of them knows,
they are not lost. They could find each other by scent
if they had to. Free of self-consciousness, they become
bodies dressed in their primitive down. What they shed
is misgiving, and in that moment deserve to be called
beautiful. A simple cleansing, the ritual way
they bathe each other to prepare for love.

She soaps him long past clean. He rinses her
with cupped hands and licks the pearls
of water at her throat. In abundance,
water slides over the rim of the tub
and they are rich for having nothing between them.

The hot sinking takes them to a place so free of longing
they could believe there was never a need
for art or music. They are surrounded by the ripple
of spaces closing, but could as well be immersed
in headwaters, framed by soft rushes,
a mud floor and the rim of the horizon.

Private Talk

What is this quarrel of body against body
this difficult fit with our loves? The uneasy and blessed
ride into the night fits perfectly into our bony terrain
like sage growing at the doorstep in a dry and sloping spot
that nothing else loves.

Its wild scent is misplaced and perfect.
And the quarrel between home and grassland
blooms purple, languid, and proves itself right
after all. What matters is skin rubbing skin, like fingers rubbing
the sage leaf, freeing the scent that makes it sage, after all.

Body longs for body, wanting him as simply as wanting
breakfast. If hunger is the great translator, I understand
the city's sad marquee that reads, "Have a private talk
with a live nude girl." In the blare of neon, this
is a whisper and what else matters, after all, but private talk.

Body clings to body and the night-blooming
orchid reels out its white tongue, divides the dark
with a path to itself. All singing comes in the name
of such generous beauty and quarrels disperse
in the scent of orchids.

At such close range, I see the fine way
the man is made, both coy and bold, like the code
of the firefly, where dark spaces mean as much
to the message as the intervals of light.

The Visit

Here are directions to their land:
On a dry day, take the road until it fans
at the top like a keyhole, then ends.
Here decide what's important and begin

carrying it across the hillside. Leave
the car behind. The hay field
climbs and dips like the back of an old horse.
At the close of summer, we see it gold and generous,

one section already baled into the shed,
most of it still waving us on. Their homestead
is another half-hour, and we hike as though
through neighborhoods—alfalfa, clover

creek bed, aspen wood, sheep pasture
in the land of handwork and barter.

All the variations—and me a stranger,
the geography of you the only familiar
sight. I fix on your strong legs and broad back
and carry my pack and spinning compass

to meet your old friends. We find them where
they've rooted, laying in for their eighteenth winter,
ready for the sympathy of snow, runoff, ground water.
We cover the years, then in the dark

hike away to the guest cabin, shuffling to be sure
we stay on the path. This one-room shelter
is wide as the bed, with one chair, a table,
and a bent trumpet on the window sill.

You bugle an old hymn down the dark valley,
letting them hear we've gone safely away.

Two Hearted River

In the best-possible world, your jacket hangs
on the empty nail in the hall and the wood floor
is tracked with water from your boots. Our cabin
rests in another peninsula, in a bend
of the Two Hearted River. I don't mind all that water,

the wash that smoothes the beach, erasing
every path. Each year there's a corner
that will not be tame, beautiful with brambles
and wild forget-me-not, buttercups
in their time. Moths roam, fluttering like the feathers
of guinea hens, but opposite—black spots on white wings.

In a still-possible world, blackness
is mediated by the white skins of birches and fall leaves
take the sun in yellow imitation. When even
the berries are gone, we'll take the fire inside our cave.

What persists will be dried blossoms,
orange with a metallic sheen that forces you back
upon your own resources. There will be reds,
catching you in the deepest value of red, five petals open,
taking the fire full on the face.

If you could stay here for just one book, turning
pages beside me evenings under a single lamp,
I would put that book in your hands and begin there,
in a language that does not tire, to build
the alphabet of our life.

Embrace

They are leaning into each other, inside
the cab of the sun bleached pickup, inside
the larger clasp of hills. The truck lurches
through ruts and the man and woman are thrown
closer as he shows where his boyhood happened.

There was my father's schoolhouse, he points at nothing,
only sagebrush and white granite. And his words are
the cinder foundation, the beams, and board nailed
to board, raised up again out of the field. When he speaks *Right by my*
she can believe that a path once wore through *house!*
the brush. Why else the convergence of dirt roads. Why else
the sudden stand of trees. She would believe him if he said
a chicken coop once stood there, or a cathedral. This is
his land, gone from barren to believable through the wild fire
of his memories.

He turns off the dirt road onto low grass where he's sure
a smaller road once was. They walk a long time
through wild sunflowers and lupine. He begins to act *7 miles from*
as if he's hearing something, pushes on as if closing in *where I grew*
on a birdcall, then stops and points at the stone monument *up.*
marking the place where one small boy was killed by a cougar.

All afternoon they drive away from the farm
then back. The hills permit the ellipse of one road, one ragged
embrace, like the specific coiling of the lover.
And the ways they have found into each other
are like this road, the soft unraveling of history, the narrow
and unguarded passage across gullies cut by sudden rainfall.
"Embrace" once meant "to set on fire."
And it could have meant to light up, like purple
fireweed against a charred hill, the luminescence
that runs back to the start. And loving someone
back to their source begins the burning.

Where we came from — the genitals.

70

Studies for the Hand and Arm of Adam

These poses are kind, the hand variously
open, reaching, or wrapped around a branch
or piece of fruit. The arm is perfectly turned
and hangs from the roundness of the shoulder,
Eve's pillow. This hand is cupped just so
for caressing a woman. The creator thought of us all
when he made a man's hand to curve this way
and laced delicacy across the tip of each finger.

Ten lifetimes ago, Durer made Adam
all over again, drew him out of the nothing
of ink and paper, and sketched a hand and arm
so beautiful, any woman would reach
toward him—especially the first one,
so perfectly alone with him.

I walk into the house, empty handed
but heavy, as though I'm carrying
something, and it is desire for you,
pulling my voice down low
and I say I want you. And you are as glad
as if no man had ever heard this before.
This humble yellow house could be
just outside the gates of Eden because there are
apples on the table, and we know what we've done.

YELLOW HOUSE AGAIN

EATEN OF THE FORBIDDEN FRUIT.

About the Author

Linda Andrews was born and raised in Detroit, and has lived for the past 25 years in Washington state. She holds a BA from Michigan State University and an MFA from the University of Washington.

Her poetry has appeared in numerous periodicals, including *Poetry Northwest, Nimrod, Seattle Review, Calyx, Willow Springs, Milkweed, Prairie Winds, Cutbank,* and *Midwest Quarterly.* She has been awarded the Richard Blessing Award, an Academy of American Poets Prize, and the Vernon M. Spence Poetry Prize.

For breadwinning purposes, she is a speechwriter, co-author and editor for healthcare executives. In this capacity, she has been published in *The Journal of Health Care Resources, American Pharmacy,* and *The New England Journal of Medicine,* among others. She is married to Dan Lamberton. Together, they have three grown children.

About the Artist

Randy LeSage is a visual artist. He works in painting, drawing, printmaking and mixed media. He has studied at Framingham State College, where he received his bachelor's degree in studio art, and at the Museum School in Boston, affiliated with Tufts University, where he earned his MFA.

He is an art instructor, currently teaching at the Worcester Art Museum. He has exhibited his artwork in museums and galleries in New England and nationally. He lives in Massachusetts.

In his own words, "I've been making art since I can remember. Along the way, I find many crossovers among artforms. Literature has been a source and influence among the creative possibilities I enjoy. Perhaps my also having been a librarian for a number of years has contributed to this aspect."